Photo Log Booklet

35m Edition - 6 exposure per table

This Photo Log Book was created by RW Jemmett to help film camera users record information about their shots including exposure, camera information and lighting. For further information about this Log Book, contact the author, access analogue photography information including film processing & supplies, check FAQs, etc. please visit

rwjemmett.com/logbook35

Published by EnergyBook - RW Jemmett

ISBN: 978-1-716-39008-1

© EnergyBook - RW Jemmett 2020

First Edition

All rights reserved. Permission is granted to copy or reprint portions for any noncommercial use, except they may not be posted online without permission.

80 tables of 6 Exposures

5x8longLuLu

How to use the Photography Log Book

This Photography Log is designed to help film/analogue photographers to record information about camera settings when out shooting. In can create a permanent record so that the photographer can understand more about the images captured and perhaps also input the information into Adobe Lightroom or similar in the future. The results should help you learn how best to use your cameras and lenses achieving better results and becoming a better photographer. It may be particularly useful when trying out a camera for the first time.

This Photo Log Book is formatted for photographers shooting analogue cameras that use 35mm film. The following notes will help you get the most from this book.

Film Make: Add the make of the film that you are using e.g. Ilford FP4 or Kodak Gold. You may also wish to add the expiry date of the film if it has already expired.

ISO: Add the speed of the film you are using e.g. 100 or 400. ISO stands for International Standards Organisation and it is a numerical value used by digital and film cameras to define the light sensitivity of the film. It can range from 25 to several thousands for digital cameras. It will always be written on the film canister/box.

Exp/Frames: Add the number of exposures/frames/shots that you expect from the film. For 35mm (135mm) film this is usually 24 or 36.

Roll: You can add a film Roll number so that you can easily reference the information in the future.

Camera Make and Model: Add some details about your camera.

Continuation: In most cases you will be using more than one table to log details about your photo shoot. So you can add 1,2,or 3. If you have more than one camera and are mixing pages up you may wish add a letter such A1, A2, A3. Or simply add Yes.

Shot/Date: The shots are numbered and it is advised that you also add a date to each shot. For continuation you may also like to add + 6. So on the continuation sheets shot 17 would be written as 11+6.

Lens mm: Add the focal length of lens that is being used. This is most helpful for cameras that have interchangeable lenses like SLRs. If a zoom is being used it is suggested that you add the actual focal length used and add the word Zoom or Z to the field. You can list the lenses used at the end of this Photo Log and reference them e.g. 2Z.

Aperture f: Add the lens aperture. Some cameras use a lens with a fixed aperture that cannot be changed. Whether fixed or variable the value is usually written on the lens.

Shutter Speed: Add the shutter speed which may be found on the lens, body of the camera or through the viewfinder. Where a longer Bulb setting is used it should be written as B2s for example.

Man/Auto Exp: Add M or A to denote whether the camera is in Manual or Auto mode. Or if you camera has several modes you may want to add Av for aperture value/priority, Sv for shutter value/priority and P for Program.

Tripod: When you view your photos later you may want to check to see if the camera was handheld or attached to a tripod when looking at the sharpness for slow Shutter speeds. You could also use HH for hand held and SUP for supported and T for timer.

Filter: If you are using an add on filter add UV, Red, Yellow, etc. You could also use this field to add information about any additional lenses such as a close-up lens e.g. CU 18ft.

Weather/Lighting: Add some information about weather lighting. For example OC for Overcast and BS for Bright Sun. This field could also be used to indicated whether a flash has been used or additional lighting such as LED lights.

Subject/Notes: The last field allows you to add further notes about the shot.You may also want to add an index to notes that you have made in the Notes section of the book. It is suggested that you reference the notes as letters (a, b, c) But you may also wish to add the film roll or page number as a reference too.

Notes

Film Make ISO Exp/Frames Roll

Camera Make & Model Continuation

Shot/Date	Lens mm	Aperture f	Shutter Speed	Man/Auto Exp	Tripod	Filter	Weather/Lighting	Subject/Notes
1								
2								
3								
4								
5								
6								

Film Make _____ ISO _____ Exp/Frames _____ Roll _____

Camera Make & Model _____ Continuation _____

Shot/Date	Lens mm	Aperture f	Shutter Speed	Man/Auto Exp	Tripod	Filter	Weather/Lighting	Subject/Notes
1								
2								
3								
4								
5								
6								

Film Make _____   ISO _____   Exp/Frames _____   Roll _____

Camera Make & Model _____   Continuation _____

Shot/Date	Lens mm	Aperture f	Shutter Speed	Man/Auto Exp	Tripod	Filter	Weather/Lighting	Subject/Notes
1								
2								
3								
4								
5								
6								

Film Make ISO Exp/Frames Roll

Camera Make & Model Continuation

Shot/Date	Lens mm	Aperture f	Shutter Speed	Man/Auto Exp	Tripod	Filter	Weather/Lighting	Subject/Notes
1								
2								
3								
4								
5								
6								

Film Make ISO Exp/Frames Roll

Camera Make & Model Continuation

Shot/Date	Lens mm	Aperture f	Shutter Speed	Man/Auto Exp	Tripod	Filter	Weather/Lighting	Subject/Notes
1								
2								
3								
4								
5								
6								

Film Make _____ ISO _____ Exp/Frames _____ Roll _____

Camera Make & Model _____ Continuation _____

Shot/Date	Lens mm	Aperture f	Shutter Speed	Man/Auto Exp	Tripod	Filter	Weather/Lighting	Subject/Notes
1								
2								
3								
4								
5								
6								

Film Make   ISO   Exp/Frames   Roll

Camera Make & Model   Continuation

Shot/Date	Lens mm	Aperture f	Shutter Speed	Man/Auto Exp	Tripod	Filter	Weather/Lighting	Subject/Notes
1								
2								
3								
4								
5								
6								

Film Make _____ ISO _____ Exp/Frames _____ Roll _____

Camera Make & Model _____ Continuation _____

Shot/Date	Lens mm	Aperture f	Shutter Speed	Man/Auto Exp	Tripod	Filter	Weather/Lighting	Subject/Notes
1								
2								
3								
4								
5								
6								

Film Make _____ ISO _____ Exp/Frames _____ Roll _____

Camera Make & Model _____ Continuation _____

Shot/Date	Lens mm	Aperture f	Shutter Speed	Man/Auto Exp	Tripod	Filter	Weather/Lighting	Subject/Notes
1								
2								
3								
4								
5								
6								

Film Make ISO Exp/Frames Roll

Camera Make & Model Continuation

Shot/Date	Lens mm	Aperture f	Shutter Speed	Man/Auto Exp	Tripod	Filter	Weather/Lighting	Subject/Notes
1								
2								
3								
4								
5								
6								

Film Make _____ ISO _____ Exp/Frames _____ Roll _____

Camera Make & Model _____ Continuation _____

Shot/Date	Lens mm	Aperture f	Shutter Speed	Man/Auto Exp	Tripod	Filter	Weather/Lighting	Subject/Notes
1								
2								
3								
4								
5								
6								

Film Make   ISO   Exp/Frames   Roll

Camera Make & Model   Continuation

Shot/Date	Lens mm	Aperture f	Shutter Speed	Man/Auto Exp	Tripod	Filter	Weather/Lighting	Subject/Notes
1								
2								
3								
4								
5								
6								

Film Make _____ ISO _____ Exp/Frames _____ Roll _____

Camera Make & Model _____ Continuation _____

Shot/Date	Lens mm	Aperture f	Shutter Speed	Man/Auto Exp	Tripod	Filter	Weather/Lighting	Subject/Notes
1								
2								
3								
4								
5								
6								

Film Make: _____ ISO: _____ Exp/Frames: _____ Roll: _____

Camera Make & Model: _____ Continuation: _____

Shot/Date	Lens mm	Aperture f	Shutter Speed	Man/Auto Exp	Tripod	Filter	Weather/Lighting	Subject/Notes
1								
2								
3								
4								
5								
6								

Film Make _____ ISO _____ Exp/Frames _____ Roll _____

Camera Make & Model _____ Continuation _____

Shot/Date	Lens mm	Aperture f	Shutter Speed	Man/Auto Exp	Tripod	Filter	Weather/Lighting	Subject/Notes
1								
2								
3								
4								
5								
6								

Film Make _____ ISO _____ Exp/Frames _____ Roll _____

Camera Make & Model _____ Continuation _____

Shot/Date	Lens mm	Aperture f	Shutter Speed	Man/Auto Exp	Tripod	Filter	Weather/Lighting	Subject/Notes
1								
2								
3								
4								
5								
6								

Film Make _____ ISO _____ Exp/Frames _____ Roll _____

Camera Make & Model _____ Continuation _____

Shot/Date	Lens mm	Aperture f	Shutter Speed	Man/Auto Exp	Tripod	Filter	Weather/Lighting	Subject/Notes
1								
2								
3								
4								
5								
6								

Film Make   ISO   Exp/Frames   Roll

Camera Make & Model   Continuation

Shot/Date	Lens mm	Aperture f	Shutter Speed	Man/Auto Exp	Tripod	Filter	Weather/Lighting	Subject/Notes
1								
2								
3								
4								
5								
6								

Film Make _____ ISO _____ Exp/Frames _____ Roll _____

Camera Make & Model _____ Continuation _____

Shot/Date	Lens mm	Aperture f	Shutter Speed	Man/Auto Exp	Tripod	Filter	Weather/Lighting	Subject/Notes
1								
2								
3								
4								
5								
6								

Film Make   ISO   Exp/Frames   Roll

Camera Make & Model   Continuation

Shot/Date	Lens mm	Aperture f	Shutter Speed	Man/Auto Exp	Tripod	Filter	Weather/Lighting	Subject/Notes
1								
2								
3								
4								
5								
6								

Film Make ISO Exp/Frames Roll

Camera Make & Model Continuation

Shot/Date	Lens mm	Aperture f	Shutter Speed	Man/Auto Exp	Tripod	Filter	Weather/Lighting	Subject/Notes
1								
2								
3								
4								
5								
6								

Film Make   ISO   Exp/Frames   Roll

Camera Make & Model   Continuation

Shot/Date	Lens mm	Aperture f	Shutter Speed	Man/Auto Exp	Tripod	Filter	Weather/Lighting	Subject/Notes
1								
2								
3								
4								
5								
6								

Film Make _____ ISO _____ Exp/Frames _____ Roll _____

Camera Make & Model _____ Continuation _____

Shot/Date	Lens mm	Aperture f	Shutter Speed	Man/Auto Exp	Tripod	Filter	Weather/Lighting	Subject/Notes
1								
2								
3								
4								
5								
6								

Film Make _____   ISO _____   Exp/Frames _____   Roll _____

Camera Make & Model _____   Continuation _____

Shot/Date	Lens mm	Aperture f	Shutter Speed	Man/Auto Exp	Tripod	Filter	Weather/Lighting	Subject/Notes
1								
2								
3								
4								
5								
6								

Film Make _____ ISO _____ Exp/Frames _____ Roll _____

Camera Make & Model _____ Continuation _____

Shot/Date	Lens mm	Aperture f	Shutter Speed	Man/Auto Exp	Tripod	Filter	Weather/Lighting	Subject/Notes
1								
2								
3								
4								
5								
6								

Film Make ISO Exp/Frames Roll

Camera Make & Model Continuation

Shot/Date	Lens mm	Aperture f	Shutter Speed	Man/Auto Exp	Tripod	Filter	Weather/Lighting	Subject/Notes
1								
2								
3								
4								
5								
6								

Film Make _____ ISO _____ Exp/Frames _____ Roll _____

Camera Make & Model _____ Continuation _____

Shot/Date	Lens mm	Aperture f	Shutter Speed	Man/Auto Exp	Tripod	Filter	Weather/Lighting	Subject/Notes
1								
2								
3								
4								
5								
6								

Film Make   ISO   Exp/Frames   Roll

Camera Make & Model   Continuation

Shot/Date	Lens mm	Aperture f	Shutter Speed	Man/Auto Exp	Tripod	Filter	Weather/Lighting	Subject/Notes
1								
2								
3								
4								
5								
6								

Film Make _____ ISO _____ Exp/Frames _____ Roll _____

Camera Make & Model _____ Continuation _____

Shot/Date	Lens mm	Aperture f	Shutter Speed	Man/Auto Exp	Tripod	Filter	Weather/Lighting	Subject/Notes
1								
2								
3								
4								
5								
6								

Film Make   ISO   Exp/Frames   Roll

Camera Make & Model   Continuation

Shot/Date	Lens mm	Aperture f	Shutter Speed	Man/Auto Exp	Tripod	Filter	Weather/Lighting	Subject/Notes
1								
2								
3								
4								
5								
6								

Film Make   ISO   Exp/Frames   Roll

Camera Make & Model   Continuation

Shot/Date	Lens mm	Aperture f	Shutter Speed	Man/Auto Exp	Tripod	Filter	Weather/Lighting	Subject/Notes
1								
2								
3								
4								
5								
6								

Film Make _____ ISO _____ Exp/Frames _____ Roll _____

Camera Make & Model _____ Continuation _____

Shot/Date	Lens mm	Aperture f	Shutter Speed	Man/Auto Exp	Tripod	Filter	Weather/Lighting	Subject/Notes
1								
2								
3								
4								
5								
6								

Film Make _____ ISO _____ Exp/Frames _____ Roll _____

Camera Make & Model _____ Continuation _____

Shot/Date	Lens mm	Aperture f	Shutter Speed	Man/Auto Exp	Tripod	Filter	Weather/Lighting	Subject/Notes
1								
2								
3								
4								
5								
6								

Film Make _____ ISO _____ Exp/Frames _____ Roll _____

Camera Make & Model _____ Continuation _____

Shot/Date	Lens mm	Aperture f	Shutter Speed	Man/Auto Exp	Tripod	Filter	Weather/Lighting	Subject/Notes
1								
2								
3								
4								
5								
6								

Film Make _____ ISO _____ Exp/Frames _____ Roll _____

Camera Make & Model _____ Continuation _____

Shot/Date	Lens mm	Aperture f	Shutter Speed	Man/Auto Exp	Tripod	Filter	Weather/Lighting	Subject/Notes
1								
2								
3								
4								
5								
6								

Film Make   ISO   Exp/Frames   Roll

Camera Make & Model   Continuation

Shot/Date	Lens mm	Aperture f	Shutter Speed	Man/Auto Exp	Tripod	Filter	Weather/Lighting	Subject/Notes
1								
2								
3								
4								
5								
6								

Film Make _____ ISO _____ Exp/Frames _____ Roll _____

Camera Make & Model _____ Continuation _____

Shot/Date	Lens mm	Aperture f	Shutter Speed	Man/Auto Exp	Tripod	Filter	Weather/Lighting	Subject/Notes
1								
2								
3								
4								
5								
6								

Film Make ISO Exp/Frames Roll

Camera Make & Model Continuation

Shot/Date	Lens mm	Aperture f	Shutter Speed	Man/Auto Exp	Tripod	Filter	Weather/Lighting	Subject/Notes
1								
2								
3								
4								
5								
6								

Film Make _____ ISO _____ Exp/Frames _____ Roll _____

Camera Make & Model _____ Continuation _____

Shot/Date	Lens mm	Aperture f	Shutter Speed	Man/Auto Exp	Tripod	Filter	Weather/Lighting	Subject/Notes
1								
2								
3								
4								
5								
6								

Film Make   ISO   Exp/Frames   Roll

Camera Make & Model   Continuation

Shot/Date	Lens mm	Aperture f	Shutter Speed	Man/Auto Exp	Tripod	Filter	Weather/Lighting	Subject/Notes
1								
2								
3								
4								
5								
6								

Film Make _____   ISO _____   Exp/Frames _____   Roll _____

Camera Make & Model _____   Continuation _____

Shot/Date	Lens mm	Aperture f	Shutter Speed	Man/Auto Exp	Tripod	Filter	Weather/Lighting	Subject/Notes
1								
2								
3								
4								
5								
6								

Film Make   ISO   Exp/Frames   Roll

Camera Make & Model   Continuation

Shot/Date	Lens mm	Aperture f	Shutter Speed	Man/Auto Exp	Tripod	Filter	Weather/Lighting	Subject/Notes
1								
2								
3								
4								
5								
6								

Film Make _____ ISO _____ Exp/Frames _____ Roll _____

Camera Make & Model _____ Continuation _____

Shot/Date	Lens mm	Aperture f	Shutter Speed	Man/Auto Exp	Tripod	Filter	Weather/Lighting	Subject/Notes
1								
2								
3								
4								
5								
6								

Film Make _____ ISO _____ Exp/Frames _____ Roll _____

Camera Make & Model _____ Continuation _____

Shot/Date	Lens mm	Aperture f	Shutter Speed	Man/Auto Exp	Tripod	Filter	Weather/Lighting	Subject/Notes
1								
2								
3								
4								
5								
6								

Film Make   ISO   Exp/Frames   Roll

Camera Make & Model   Continuation

Shot/Date	Lens mm	Aperture f	Shutter Speed	Man/Auto Exp	Tripod	Filter	Weather/Lighting	Subject/Notes
1								
2								
3								
4								
5								
6								

Film Make   ISO   Exp/Frames   Roll

Camera Make & Model   Continuation

Shot/Date	Lens mm	Aperture f	Shutter Speed	Man/Auto Exp	Tripod	Filter	Weather/Lighting	Subject/Notes
1								
2								
3								
4								
5								
6								

Film Make   ISO   Exp/Frames   Roll

Camera Make & Model   Continuation

Shot/Date	Lens mm	Aperture f	Shutter Speed	Man/Auto Exp	Tripod	Filter	Weather/Lighting	Subject/Notes
1								
2								
3								
4								
5								
6								

Film Make　　　　ISO　　　　Exp/Frames　　　　Roll

Camera Make & Model　　　　Continuation

Shot/Date	Lens mm	Aperture f	Shutter Speed	Man/Auto Exp	Tripod	Filter	Weather/Lighting	Subject/Notes
1								
2								
3								
4								
5								
6								

Film Make _____ ISO _____ Exp/Frames _____ Roll _____

Camera Make & Model _____ Continuation _____

Shot/Date	Lens mm	Aperture f	Shutter Speed	Man/Auto Exp	Tripod	Filter	Weather/Lighting	Subject/Notes
1								
2								
3								
4								
5								
6								

Film Make **ISO** **Exp/Frames** **Roll**

Camera Make & Model **Continuation**

Shot/Date	Lens mm	Aperture f	Shutter Speed	Man/Auto Exp	Tripod	Filter	Weather/Lighting	Subject/Notes
1								
2								
3								
4								
5								
6								

Film Make _____ ISO _____ Exp/Frames _____ Roll _____

Camera Make & Model _____ Continuation _____

Shot/Date	Lens mm	Aperture f	Shutter Speed	Man/Auto Exp	Tripod	Filter	Weather/Lighting	Subject/Notes
1								
2								
3								
4								
5								
6								

Film Make _____ ISO _____ Exp/Frames _____ Roll _____

Camera Make & Model _____ Continuation _____

Shot/Date	Lens mm	Aperture f	Shutter Speed	Man/Auto Exp	Tripod	Filter	Weather/Lighting	Subject/Notes
1								
2								
3								
4								
5								
6								

Film Make _____ ISO _____ Exp/Frames _____ Roll _____

Camera Make & Model _____ Continuation _____

Shot/Date	Lens mm	Aperture f	Shutter Speed	Man/Auto Exp	Tripod	Filter	Weather/Lighting	Subject/Notes
1								
2								
3								
4								
5								
6								

Film Make   ISO   Exp/Frames   Roll

Camera Make & Model   Continuation

Shot/Date	Lens mm	Aperture f	Shutter Speed	Man/Auto Exp	Tripod	Filter	Weather/Lighting	Subject/Notes
1								
2								
3								
4								
5								
6								

Film Make   ISO   Exp/Frames   Roll

Camera Make & Model   Continuation

Shot/Date	Lens mm	Aperture f	Shutter Speed	Man/Auto Exp	Tripod	Filter	Weather/Lighting	Subject/Notes
1								
2								
3								
4								
5								
6								

Film Make _____ ISO _____ Exp/Frames _____ Roll _____

Camera Make & Model _____ Continuation _____

Shot/Date	Lens mm	Aperture f	Shutter Speed	Man/Auto Exp	Tripod	Filter	Weather/Lighting	Subject/Notes
1								
2								
3								
4								
5								
6								

Film Make   ISO   Exp/Frames   Roll

Camera Make & Model   Continuation

Shot/Date	Lens mm	Aperture f	Shutter Speed	Man/Auto Exp	Tripod	Filter	Weather/Lighting	Subject/Notes
1								
2								
3								
4								
5								
6								

Film Make   **ISO**   **Exp/Frames**   **Roll**

Camera Make & Model   **Continuation**

Shot/Date	Lens mm	Aperture f	Shutter Speed	Man/Auto Exp	Tripod	Filter	Weather/Lighting	Subject/Notes
1								
2								
3								
4								
5								
6								

Film Make _____ ISO _____ Exp/Frames _____ Roll _____

Camera Make & Model _____ Continuation _____

Shot/Date	Lens mm	Aperture f	Shutter Speed	Man/Auto Exp	Tripod	Filter	Weather/Lighting	Subject/Notes
1								
2								
3								
4								
5								
6								

Film Make   ISO   Exp/Frames   Roll

Camera Make & Model   Continuation

Shot/Date	Lens mm	Aperture f	Shutter Speed	Man/Auto Exp	Tripod	Filter	Weather/Lighting	Subject/Notes
1								
2								
3								
4								
5								
6								

Film Make _____ ISO _____ Exp/Frames _____ Roll _____

Camera Make & Model _____ Continuation _____

Shot/Date	Lens mm	Aperture f	Shutter Speed	Man/Auto Exp	Tripod	Filter	Weather/Lighting	Subject/Notes
1								
2								
3								
4								
5								
6								

Film Make   ISO   Exp/Frames   Roll

Camera Make & Model   Continuation

Shot/Date	Lens mm	Aperture f	Shutter Speed	Man/Auto Exp	Tripod	Filter	Weather/Lighting	Subject/Notes
1								
2								
3								
4								
5								
6								

Film Make   ISO   Exp/Frames   Roll

Camera Make & Model   Continuation

Shot/Date	Lens mm	Aperture f	Shutter Speed	Man/Auto Exp	Tripod	Filter	Weather/Lighting	Subject/Notes
1								
2								
3								
4								
5								
6								

Film Make _____ ISO _____ Exp/Frames _____ Roll _____

Camera Make & Model _____ Continuation _____

Shot/Date	Lens mm	Aperture f	Shutter Speed	Man/Auto Exp	Tripod	Filter	Weather/Lighting	Subject/Notes
1								
2								
3								
4								
5								
6								

Abbreviations:

Abbreviation	Description

Sunny 16 Rule

The Sunny 16 Rule is a way to obtain the correct exposure in daylight without using a camera's meter or a light meter.

The basic rule states that if you have a clear, sunny day and your aperture is at f/16, you should set your shutter speed to one over the ISO of the film that you are using. So if you are using ISO 200 film at f/16, then your shutter speed will be 1/200 second. If your ISO is 100 then you should set your shutter speed at 1/100 second. If you do not have these exact shutter speed settings on your camera (i.e. you have 1/250s instead of 1/200) do not worry, just use the closest setting available.

You can then adjust the aperture to reflect the actual lighting conditions for the shot by using the table below.

Aperture	Lighting Conditions	Shadow Detail
f/22	Snow/sand	Dark with sharp edges
f/16	Sunny	Distinct
f/11	Slight overcast	Soft around edges
f/8	Overcast	Barely Visible
f/5.6	Heavy overcast	No shadows
f/4	Open shade/sunset	No shadows

If you identify the right aperture from the table above you can then change other exposure settings by making sure that you always change both the aperture and the shutter speed as follows.

Let us say you're shooting at f16 with an ISO of 200 and a shutter speed of 1/200, but you want to open the aperture to f/11. Since f11 is a larger aperture than f16 by one stop (+1 EV), you will have to compensate and go down one stop (-1 EV) with the shutter speed to maintain the same exposure. That means that at f11, you would set a shutter speed of 1/400 second to get the same exposure as you did using f16 and a shutter speed of 1/200 second, assuming the ISO stays the same at 200 in both situations. (With a digital camera you could choose to change the ISO).

When you are shooting film the accepted rule is - if in doubt, overexpose. Colour print and Black and White film have a large latitude for overexposure. If you have your negatives scanned you can use post editing (Lightroom, Photoshop, Affinity Photo, Pixelmator, GIMP, etc) to correct the image with minimal loss of information.

This Log Book was designed and published by RW Jemmett.

Find out more about this Log Book

rwjemmett.com/logbook35

This Log Book belongs to.

Name:

Contact:

Log Book Number:

Dates: From　　　　　　　　　To

Cameras Used:

1
2
3
4
5
6

Lenses Used:

1
2
3
4
5

www.ingramcontent.com/pod-product-compliance
Lightning Source LLC
Chambersburg PA
CBHW021506210526
45463CB00002B/912